The Sea S

The #1 Guide to Maritime Law, Nautical Issues, & Private Ocean Disputes

by

Austin Robinson, LLM
Connor Gleim, PhD
Patrick Golden, GNP

Copyright © 2019 Sea Section Law, Incorporated

www.potholepress.com

All rights reserved

Book design by Rebecca

First published on January 14th, 2019

ISBN:
978-0-9992029-4-4

THIS BOOK IS DEDICATED TO OUR LOVE: THE SEA

NOTE: ALL PROCEEDS FROM THE SALES OF THIS BOOK WILL BE DONATED STRAIGHT TO LONELY WHALE FOUNDATION, A NONPROFIT ORGANIZATION BASED IN THE UNITED STATES DEDICATED TO BRINGING PEOPLE CLOSER TO THE WORLD'S OCEANS THROUGH EDUCATION AND AWARENESS, INSPIRING EMPATHY AND ACTION FOR OCEAN HEALTH AND THE WELLBEING OF MARINE WILDLIFE.

LEARN MORE ABOUT LONELY WHALE FOUNDATION HERE: WWW.SEASECTION.ORG

TABLE OF CONTENTS

ACKNOWLEDGMENTS

We would like to acknowledge Marshall
Dahng Geyer for giving us the hope and
willpower and money to complete this novel.
So much money. Like, a sea of money. We
love you, Marshall. Thank you.

1
ALL ABOARD!

"The Sea is the wisest of men, the most beautiful of women, and the dirtiest of animals."

- Scott von Dilnderhurst

NOTE: The sole point of this chapter is to recount the authors' experiences with the sea. If you would like to learn more about Maritime Law, it is best to skip this chapter. Although, who knows, you may just find inspiration in our stories and get into Maritime Law if you haven't already!

<u>Connor</u>

After my fifth divorce, I decided to set sail to the sea. You see, the sea had never let me down before. She was a loyal companion to me – always there, always fair. Sure, there were times she would become temperamental and capsize my boat, leaving me stranded in the middle of the Atlantic ocean praying to whichever god would listen... but she always called out to the surrounding boats, sending waves to bring them to my rescue. Not like Misty – my ex-wife – who probably would have just tied a sack of rocks to my leg and helped me drown. No, the sea always made sure I was safe. I knew deep down that the sea was always the wife I never had. My sixth wife. That was, of course, until I met Deb – my real sixth wife.

I was 40 years old when I decided to attend the best nautical institution in the world: The World Admiralty University (WAU) in Sweden! After a long series of failed career attempts – political comptroller, home masonry repair man, ghostwriter; just to name a few – I wanted to become a researcher and master of the sea! I have been sailing since I was just a little baby. My mother even claims that I came out of her womb in a sailor outfit on a Lake Freighter screaming "AHOY, MATEY!" while fighting off Somalian pirates. This, of course, is ridiculous to imagine, but if you know me, you know that it is much more realistic than how a baby naturally comes out!

During my first semester at WAU, I met this wonderful woman named Debruary – Deb for short. She sat next to me in Let's Get Naut-y, a class taught by Professor Christina Boatman. The course was an intro-level one to mine and Deb's Ocean Pollution track of our graduate degree. The moment I fell in love with her was when she leaned over to me and said, "Can you believe all of the junk humans throw into our beautiful seas? Maritime? More like MariCRIME!"

From there, it was smooth sailing. I received a 4.0 GPA, graduated at the top of my class right under Deb, worked with the United Nations to secure better Maritime Law codes in Scandinavia, and fell in love with the sea even more. At the age of 45, I will be presenting my research regarding the United Nations' Convention on the Law of the Ocean! And who knows, there may even be mini Connor and Debruary Gleims on the way ;)

Austin

Cape Breton Island. That's where it all began. My first kiss, my first sip of alcohol, my first touch of the sea. When I was just six years old, my father – a single parent – would get on the ferry in Sydney, Nova Scotia every day searching for my mother, who was swallowed up by the waves while on their way back from Newfoundland. And I was right beside him.

My mother gave birth to me on the ferry while it was making its way back from Argentia, Newfoundland. My parents had an affinity for St. John's and spent their honeymoon there after performing a shotgun wedding on Signal Hill. She tried to hold off giving birth to me until they reached the shores of Nova Scotia. And she was almost successful. Until an elderly couple on the ferry noticed that her water broke about 52 kilometers out – everyone else assumed a big wave had just gotten her coochie wet. Suddenly, she was giving birth to a beautiful baby boy: Me.

Anyway, I stood by my father's side as we took that ferry every single day for five years:

from my ages of six to eleven. He really thought she was still out there. Waiting.

I didn't start school until I was 12 years old. I was much older than the other Kindergarteners. By the time I was in Grade 1, I was a teenager. I turned 18 the day I started Grade 6. You get where I'm going with this: I was out of place for most of my life. Graduating secondary school at the age of 24 is not something you easily get over. Sure, my classmates were jealous of my facial hair and chest hair in Grade 4, I easily became the national champion of the Canada National Water Polo League for five years in a row, and I was legally allowed to have sex with my teachers in high school. But there were many downfalls, too. Sarah – my girlfriend in 3rd grade – broke up with me after her parents got wind of how old I was (15), and maintaining a fast food job without having learned multiplication yet was pretty tough. But I made it through. And I kept my eye on the prize: suing the ocean to avenge my mother's death.

Once I knew I wanted to take the entire sea to court, I had my college plans. I went to

Dollhouse University in Halifax. Throughout my entire Maritime Law program, my professors and peers told me I was stupid and that I couldn't pursue legal action against a large body of water that takes up 71% of our planet and is responsible for the Water Cycle. But I knew better. Now look at me! I'm a Maritime Lawyer appealing his case against the ocean over and over again until the Supreme Court takes it on!

Patrick
    I just love water.

2
THE HISTORY
OF MARITIME LAW

"A minute at sea is worth more than a lifetime on land."

- John John Bornstanstein

Maritime Law – or Admiralty Law – has an incredibly long and complex history. Although it seems this form of law would have been discovered when most ships and boats were traveling around, it actually began between 600 and 800 AD as a subset of Byzantine Law. *Nomos Rhodion Nautikos*, English for Rhodian Sea Law – or The Sea Law, – were a collection of maritime rules and regulations that the Romans created in three parts:

1. The ratification of Naval Law under the Roman Emperors,
2. The participation and regulations available to the crew of the vessel, and
3. Who's responsible for the theft or damage of the cargo being carried.

However, these written documents from over a millennia ago did not survive the passage of time and, thus, are no longer available to us except in the form of thoughts and assumptions. In actuality, we receive more insight regarding Rhodian Sea Law from other Byzantine and Roman Empire legal documents and codes than from the original documents themselves.

Although long lost, these documents are not forgotten. Many other empires, countries, and governmental entities looked toward Rhodian Sea Law throughout the years for guidance and advice on how to handle nautical issues and open ocean disputes. For example, Southern Italy erected the Ordinamenta et consuetudo maris – or the

Ordinances and Custom of the Sea – in Trani during the year 1063. Although it is not the oldest maritime law code, it is the oldest existing one to have survived and in which we can reference. Shortly after, Italy also founded the Amalfian Laws: a set of maritime law codes compiled in the 12th century and used for centuries to model other international mercantile codes as they related to the sea.

Although Amalfian Laws were widely and vastly influential, it is the former set of Italian maritime law codes that we set sale to. The Ordinances and Custom of the Sea started out as a convention that governed maritime trade back in the 11th century. The law codes along with how the convention went were preserved in a Venetian version attached to the *Statuta Firmanorum* in 1507. Luckily, there are multiple versions so future Maritime Lawyers and Researchers (such as Robinson and Gleim) will have a copy, unlike with Rhodian Sea Law. Although the text of the Ordinances and Custom of the Sea were originally put into question for authenticity, the fact that the documents were label with the year 1063 is foolproof against the naysayers. Along with

Rhodian Sea Law, this document and historic sea code proves that Maritime Law has been around and has been highly influential for a very long time.

Only three years after the Ordinances and Custom of the Sea, Maritime Law began being used as an alternate set of codes to Common Law in England during the Norman Conquest. This substitution use led to the French Queen Eleanor of Aquitaine becoming a primary advocate for the law, as well as her exposure to the law while crusading the eastern Mediterranean. The Queen liked Maritime Law to such an extent that she decided to establish a set of codes on the island of Oleron, under the document "Rolls of Oleron". After discovering the success of this set of codes on the island, the Queen decided to establish the law back into the country of England once again. This reestablishment of the law led to a special court being created in the country: Admiralty Court.

This court was stagnant more or less in England until the year 1750, when the industrial revolution created much use for the court. Not only was there more productivity in the courts, they become a source of elaborate legal dreams and inventive provisions that could be abused due to the new situation the world was going through. Due to the abuse and exploitation the courts were receiving, they were abolished by the Judicature Acts of 1873-1875 and added to the High Court as a lesser entity with minimal power under the "Probate, Divorce & Admiralty" (PDA) division. However, shortly after, the PDA division was also abolished and Admiralty Court was included in simply "Family Division" in the High Court.

The English use of Maritime Law was actually quite important for the eventual American Revolution that happened between 1765 and 1783. The writing in the Declaration of Independence "For depriving us in many cases, of benefits of Trial by Jury" was influenced by the UK Parliament in regard to granting the Admiralty Courts jurisdiction to enforce The Stamp Act in the English colonies within the country that would later become known as The United States of America. The reason this was so influential during the revolution is because The Stamp Act was wildly opposed in the colonies, so much in fact that the juries would often ignore any case of a colonist being in violation of the act.

Although pre-country United States despised the Maritime Laws proposed on them by the English, they did become part of the law of the country gradually. Once the U.S. Constitution was adopted in 1789, Admiralty become all the rage, creating many lawyers who focused solely on Maritime Law. One of these very prominent lawyers was Alexander Hamilton himself! However, right before the creation of the country, in 1787 John Adams wrote to James Madison that he should amend the constitution clause that stated

"...trial by jury in all matters of fact triable by the laws of the land and not by the laws of Nations."

to

"...trial by jury in all matters of fact

triable by the laws of the land as opposed the law of admiralty and not by the laws of Nations, i.e. not by the law of admiralty."

The result? The Seventh Amendment to the United States Constitution.

Although there are countless tales and facts we could provide about the history of Maritime Law, those presented in this chapter are the most important in your studies.

3
THE FEATURES
OF MARTIME LAW

"My life, my lady, my lover... is the sea!"

- Hannah 'Sea Loving' Winokur

So, you may be wondering, what exactly does Maritime Law entail? You know the history of Maritime Law, you know our stories with Maritime Law, but what exactly does Maritime Law contain? What are some of the features? Who needs to be sued and what needs to be done to bring on such suage when it regards Maritime Law? This chapter is all about just that: the features of Maritime Law.

In this chapter, we lay out five different characteristics of Maritime Law. These characteristics are incredibly important, as a lot of questions can be raised when it comes to this type of law. What happens if a seaman gets injured while on a ship in international waters? Which country is responsible for the care of passengers on a cruise ship while it's sailing across the Pacific? Can banks put a lien on a ship that spends most of its time in stateless territories? What happens when a ship is lost at sea or need to be properly salvaged? What are the laws on pollution out at sea? Exactly how much of the ocean does each seaside country own? Why do all of these questions seem so hazy and almost unanswerable? Well, we're going to try out best through explaining the following:

- Maintenance & Cure: The required amount of care, services, and obligations the shipowner has to their seamen.
- Passenger Injuries: The reasonable care owed to the passengers of a ship, along with how exactly persons can take action against a ship in international

waters.

- Liens & Mortgages on Ships: How and when banks can loan money to the owners of ships, and what it means when those loans are paid back.
- Treasure Salvage: What happens when property is lost at sea, rescued at sea, or even pirated at sea.
- Ocean Ownership: How much of the sea each water-touching country owns. Hint: it's complicated.

We will now present a quick overview of all four of these important characteristics that are imperative to Maritime Law. Although there are many, many more characteristics within the set of nautical codes, these four make up the cornerstones of the law.

Maintenance & Cure

The ideology of marine maintenance and cure begins with Article VI of the Rolls of Oleron – the document stated earlier that was sponsored and championed by Queen

Eleanor of Aquitaine in 1160 AD. By cure, the document meant that a shipowner is required to provide medical care for free to the workers of the ship that happened to get injured while servicing the ship. Not only must the shipowner cure their employees, but they must do so until the employees have received the maximum medical cure possible. Although this sounds all good and dandy, this simply means the injured must be cured – not necessarily improved. If a worker contracts scabies while working for the ship, the employer simply has the obligation to cure the scabies, not necessarily the complications that come along with scabies. Although, this form of cure does include providing the injured with the proper medication and medical devices required to improving the ability to function – even if that includes long term treatments.

The idea of maintenance has more to do with the quality of life of the injured seamen than the idea of cure. Maintenance covers the seamen with basic living expenses while they are getting better and back to their usual duties of cruising the sea and performing their ship duties. However, the obligation of maintenance from the shipowner is over the second the employee is able to start working once again. Although it is important to note that the seaman may lose their right to maintenance while the right to cure is still continuing.

Of course, not all shipowners may be ethical and accepting of these obligations and seamen rights. If a ship worker is not given proper maintenance and cure, they may sue a shipowner to recover their rights. Likewise, they may recover the maritime attorney fees in the process. Ultimately, the shipowner may be subject to punitive damages, according to Atlantic Sounding Co. v. Townsend, 557 U.S. 404, if they breach their obligations to provide maintenance and cure.

Passenger Injuries

The idea behind the passenger injuries is that shipowners have an obligation to provide reasonable care to their passengers. However, if a passenger is injured while on a ship –

regardless of whether or not it is currently sailing in international waters – they may sue the shipowner as if they are on land by pledging negligence of a third party. It is the passengers responsibility to prove that the shipowner was indeed negligent if this is the case. The passenger has up to three years to pursue this case if on a regular ship, or only one year if on a ship owned by a cruise line. The latter is in place given the fact that the passenger has a purchased ticket, and also requires that the passenger place notice of the lawsuit to the company up to six months after exiting the ship. Regardless of when the case is brought up (as long as in the time limit), most major cruise ships – at least in the United States of America – require that the suit be placed in the city of either Miami, Florida or Seattle, Washington.

However, just as law goes, sometimes the victim doesn't always win. In 1954 – in the case Adler v. Dickson (The Himalaya) – a shipping line was able to dodge liability after a passenger was injured. In this case, even though the victim was indeed injured while on the ship, the shipowner was protected by an exemption clause posted on the purchased ticket by the passenger. The shipping line was completely absolved of liability simply from writing a little sentence on the ticket. Since then, the Unfair Contract Terms Act 1977 was created in order to make it illegal for shipping lines to absolve themselves of liability for death or passenger injuries caused by their negligence.

Liens & Mortgages on Ships:

Who are those who have a lien against the ship? There are several parties that can have a lien – literal or otherwise – on the ship: banks which loan money in order for the owner to purchase the ship, vendors who supply the owner with necessities like fuel and stores, the ship workers who need any outstanding pay, and many more. These parties have a lien to guarantee payment. However, in order for one of these parties to enforce the lien, the ship must first be seized or arrested. Furthermore, if the enforcement of the lien happens against a ship from the United States, the case must be brought in a federal court – not a state court. The only exception in this case is under the reverse-Erie doctrine, which allows the state courts to apply federal law.

An interesting rule seen in Maritime Law, that is not seen in most laws consisting of liens, is that any maritime lienholder immediately have superiority over any other type of lienholder, even if that lienholder came first in the equation. In fact all maritime lienholders are completely superior in regard to all aspects when it comes to Maritime Law.

The specific reasons for a shipowner to receive a maritime lien are as follows:
- Wages of the ship's workers
- The operations of salvage
- General average claims
- Claims for the breach of a charter party
- Ship mortgages
- Claims under maritime contracts for repairs, supplies, towage, pilotage, and a wide variety of other necessaries
- Claims for maritime torts including personal injury and death, and collision claims
- Claims for the damage or loss of cargo

- Claim by the carrier of cargo for unpaid freight and demurrage
- Pollution claims

This list also changes depending on the country the ship is from. For example, in the United Kingdom bunker suppliers are not protected by maritime lien. Although, the opposite is true in the United States.

So how does one distinguish between a shipowner's lien and a maritime lien? Although some authorities don't acknowledge a difference between the two, most believe that the former is a possessory lien, which marks the primary difference. However, the right to this type of lien can only be applies on goods which are delivered by the shipowner when the shipper is the contractual party.

In order to discharge the lien from a ship, the owner must pay the claims, waiver, laches, foreclosure, and sales connected to the ship. If the lienholder requests to waive the lien, it should be clearly outline by the requirement of the court — and only after that will the credit of the lienholder be considered. If the lienholder fails to have the ship arrested within a specific amount of time, it may result in the cancellation of the original claim. However, this is ultimately determined on a case-by-case basis. After all is said and done, the lienholder needs to show that they exercised due diligence when attempting to take action with their lien. If a shipowner decides to engage in an international sale of their ship, they have the right to remove the attachment of the lien and receive a clear title. Lastly, the lien is eliminated if the entire ship is destroyed. Not partial destruction, but whole destruction. The lien can still be attached to the remaining part of the vessel if partially destroyed.

Treasure Salvage:

Oh! The good part! Treasure! Not that kind of treasure, silly! We're talking about Marine Salvage! Although, to us, this is the best type of treasure there is!

When someone loses property out at sea and it is rescued by another person, a salvage award is in order. However, this does not extend to saving the life of another human being – if someone saves your life while you are at sea, you are not required to present them with a salvage award or any type of award. That is why salvage law only applies to the saving of property. That being said, there are two types of salvage: contract salvage and pure salvage.

Contract Salvage: The property owner and the person who salvaged the property enter into a contract prior to the exchange of the award and the return of the salvage. The award – typically a monetary amount – is determined by the contract.

Pure Salvage: While there is no contractual agreement in this case, there is an understood agreement implied by law. The person who salvages the property takes it to court and is awarded based on merit of the service and how valuable the property is worth. This can be done in one of two ways: high-order and low-order. When something has a high-order salvage importance, it means that typically the person who salvaged the property did so at the risk of themselves and their crew members / their own property. For example, if they are saving a sinking ship, they run of the risk of drowning. When something has low-order salvage importance, it means that there was very little to no risk of anyone's life or property in the salvage operation. An example of this would be towing a vessel. Regardless of the order of importance, the salvor is given an award based upon the value of the property saved.

A pure salvage award typically consists of 50% of the value of the property saved or below. Unless, of course, it is a treasure salvage. Even if the original owner is still alive when their sunken treasure is found, the salvor will still get a majority of the value considering it would possibly never have been found without them in the first place. Valuable sunken treasure can include sunken ships from various countries, war ships from the past, merchant ships, and much more.

Although making treasure salvage a way of life would be expensive to get into, it could pay off in the long run.

Ocean Ownership:

So, who owns the ocean? If someone owns the land we stand on and the cities we reside in, then who owns the water surrounding us? Although we all seem to experience governing bodies taking control of almost every aspect of our life, our sea is not one of them. That means that 71% of our world is ungoverned and cannot be politicized.

Or can they? Although it's true for the most part that our ocean cannot be governed, part of it can be. Each country is allowed 12 miles from their shore of governable water. This means that the country can impose any law they want on those 12 miles of water and all domestic rules apply. This is known as "Territorial Waters" to the country, and it can be crossed by ships from other countries as long as they are doing so innocently (i.e. not fishing, trading weapons, etc.).

It doesn't stop there. The next 12 miles are known to its country as "The Contiguous Zone". So far we are up to 24 miles of ocean water that each country is able to own.

However, the second 12 miles can only be utilized if the country is wanting to enforce customers, taxation, immigration, or pollution. Beyond those 24 miles, there are 200 nautical miles (230 miles) given to each country called the "Exclusive Economic Zone" (EEZ). The only benefit this gives the country is that it is allowed to harvest natural resources within their EEZ. Therefore, a seaside country technically owns 254 miles of water from its shore.

So what if two seaside countries are very close to each other? Good questions. This happened in the South China Sea, a very important spot on the map for resources, traveling, and shipping. Numerous countries touching this sea claim they own water that other countries are claiming, as well. The very loose correction to this is to have all of the countries agree to a line in between each other them. Of course, this requires that the countries work together and agree upon a solution, which is not so easily done. Most countries will split the line down the middle, but when you have a lot of countries involved and the resources are at stake, it can result in some pretty nasty tensions.

Now although countries can own all of this water, they cannot enforce their own domestic laws upon travelers until the travelers are in the first 12 miles – or the Territorial Zone – of the country. That means that the laws of the country the ship is from is the law that's on the ship up to the point it reaches a territorial zone. That also means that a baby born on a cruise ship in the territorial zone waters of the United States will receive U.S. citizenship. Although not every country abides by citizenship on soil, and there are some exceptions to this rules. Likewise, the United National during their Convention on The Reduction of Statelessness – something we will get into later in the next chapter – concluded that babies that are born in international waters should simply take the nationality of their parents. This sounds fair and easy enough, except for the fact that there are countries that do not grant citizenship due to blood line. In this case, the baby will simply have the citizenship of the country in which the ship is registered. You can have a child be a Panama citizen without ever having been there or having any ancestors there whatsoever! That's pretty wild.

So if a Panama ship has Panama laws, then does that mean I could jump on a Canadian ship and legally smoke pot? Actually, yes! Fortunately and unfortunately, Maritime Laws are easily and widely exploited in this way. During the United States Prohibition era, U.S. ships often changed their registration to be in different countries so that they could get away with serving and drinking alcohol. This also happened with gambling!

So there you have it: the features of Maritime Law. Do you see why we love this type of law and research now? Do you understand why it has such a long and complicated history? Well, luckily our next chapter covers the future of admiralty and the variety of international conventions that have happened thanks to the confusion Maritime Law brings! So buckle in! And yes, some boats do have seatbelts ;)

4
SETTING SAIL...
TO CONVENTIONS!

"A, B, Sea, D."

- Alexander Walrus

Ah, conventions. Like a school of fish coming together to learn about their environment. Instead they're humans, and not fish. And it's not their environment, it's the ocean. And it's a lot like school because people are learning!

Anyway, before 1897, international conventions regarding maritime law virtually didn't exist. It wasn't until a private organization comprised of maritime lawyers came along and decided to draft numerous conventions focusing on the law of the sea. They called themselves the Comité Maritime International (International Maritime Committee in English, CMI in acronym) and create conventions on a wide variety of topics relating to the ocean, including the Hague Rules and the Salvage Convention.

It wasn't until 1958 that another Maritime organization was created to take over the functions of CMI: the International Maritime Organization (IMO). This time, it was created by one of the most powerful organizations in the world: The United Nations. Omg this book was written in one day, are you seriously still reading this? However, the IMO did not become effective until 1974. With international conventions such as "the International Convention for the Safety of Life at Sea" (SOLAS), "the Standards for Training, Certification, and Watchkeeping" (STCW), the "International Regulations for Preventing Collisions at Sea" (COLREGS), "Maritime Pollution Regulations" (MARPOL), "International Aeronautical and Maritime Search and Rescue Convention"

(IAMSAR), the IMO quickly became the leading convention organization about maritime boundaries, the marine environment, and the law of the sea. To understand more about what the IMO conventions accomplish, we need to dive into a couple of these conventions.

The United Nations Convention on the Law of the Sea:

The United Nations Convention on the Law of the Sea was prompted by the people's desire to settle the issues pertaining to the law of the sea as it relates to the maintenance of peace, justice, and progress for the world. The convention held the belief that the problems of ocean space are all interconnected and need to be considered as a whole. Ultimately, the convention wanted to establish a legal order for the seas and the oceans that will ensure international communication; protect and preserve the marine environment; and promote peacefulness, equity, and efficiently utilize resources. Through the achievement of these goals, the convention hoped that it would contribute to the world's realization of a better international economic order as it relates to humankind's needs and interests as a whole – especially bearing in mind those of developing countries.

The parties who have the right to sign the convention documents are those recognized by the UN as intergovernmental organizations that have been given competence over the matters regarding the convention by their governmental state. Said parties must have the majority of its members present at the convention in order to make a declaration regarding the convention matters. The same goes for if the parties want to amend or ratify part of the convention documents.

The third United Nations Conference on the Law of the Sea ended in 3 annexations and 4 resolutions to the official documents.

The United Nations Convention on the Reduction of Statelessness:

The United Nations Convention on the Reduction of Statelessness was adopted on August 30th, 1961 and set out to reduced statelessness – primarily in relation to the oceans – by international agreement. There were 21 articles and they are as follows:

1. A governmental body must grants its nationality to a baby born in its territory if it would otherwise be stateless.
   a. The governmental body must grant its nationality in accordance to several conditions: within 18 and 21 years, certain residency requirements, without concerns of convictions, etc.
   b. The child born in a stateless area may take on the nationality of the state that the mother was born in.
   c. Clarifications on sub-articles a-c.
   d. Clarifications on sub-articles a-c.
2. A child found in the territory of an agreeing state shall be considered to have that territory's nationality.
3. If a child is born on a ship while in

stateless waters, the child shall be given the nationality of the flag that flies on the boat or wherever the boat is registered.

4. An agreeing state may grant its nationality to someone who would be stateless if one of the person's parents is a citizen of that state. Nationality may be granted:

   a. At birth, or

   b. After an application is filed.

5. The only way a stateless person given nationality can lose said nationality is if the agreeing state has a condition on a change in personal status, such as marriage, divorce, adoption, etc. And even then, the only way nationality can be revoked is if the stateless person has obtained another nationality. And even after that, the previously-stateless person must be given an opportunity to recover the nationality by written application to the governing body.

6. Clarifications on article 6.

7. The previously stateless person cannot denounce their nationality unless they

acquire another nationality.

    a. Some states that have given nationality to stateless persons have a rule that once the person has lived abroad for seven or more years (and has another nationality), they must denounce the nationality of the state.

    b. However, this person could retain their nationality if they declare their intent to the appropriate authority of the state and the state agree.

    c. Ultimately, the person will not lose their nationality if the lose of it would render them stateless.

8. The state may not deprive a person of nationality if doing so would make the person stateless.

9. A state may not deprive a person of nationality on grounds of race, ethnicity, religion, or politics.

10. Every treaty between two or more states that discusses the transfer of nationality is required to provide a provision designed to secure that a person will not become stateless as a

result of the transfer.

11. All agreeing states must promote the establishment of these rules and laws within the framework of the United Nations.

12. Agreeing states that don't usually grant soil birth nationality must follow all provisions of this convention for people born before and after these documents.

13. The conventions provisions will not affect any state provisions that happen to be more effective for the reduction of statelessness.

14. If two or more agreeing states need to settle a dispute between themselves as it relates to the realm of statelessness, it can be settled by the International Court of Justice at the request of any of the parties.

15. The convention applies to all territories that are non-self-governing, colonized, and owned by states that have agreed to the convention.

    a. In the case that the territory of an agreeing state is not completely non-self-governing or colonized and the state cannot make definite decisions for them, the state must gain consent from the territory before the convention and its provisions can be applies.

b. This must be done within 12 months.

16. This convention is open for signatures from states at the United Nations' Headquarters from August 30th, 1961 to May 31st, 1962.

a. Signatures are accepted from any state member of the UN.

b. Signatures are accepted from any state invited to attend the conference.

c. Propositions to ratify any of the articles of this convention should be addressed to the Secretary-General of the UN.

17. Ratification requests must be made during the signature timeframe.

18. The convention documents and the signatures will enter into force a full two years after the signature timeframe has concluded.

19. If a non-metropolitan territory governed by one of the agreeing states has a concern, they must do so as their own entity.
20. The Secretary-General of the UN will notify all member states of signatures, ratifications, accessions, reservations, dates, and denunciations.
21. The convention will be registered by the Secretary-General of the UN on the date of its entry into force.

Now that you know more about what these conventions accomplish and do, it's time to discuss what some of the current issues are in the United Nation's International Maritime Organization as of January 2019. Recent initiative include amending the International Convention for the Safety of Life at Sea and the International Convention on Standards of Training, Certification, and Watchkeeping for Seafarers. Likewise, the IMO has taken on a role in tackling climate change! It participated in the 2015 United Nations Climate Change Conference in Paris.

It hopes to reduce maritime greenhouse emissions expected to last until 2020. The IMO is also responsible for recently publishing the International Code of Signals between merchants and naval vessels. It created a traffic service called e-Navigation, which it is still working on. Stay tuned for Maritime Domain Awareness!

5
NEXT DESTINATION:
THE WORLD!

"You see is what you see. But what I see is sea."

- Elon Musk (no, not that one!)

This chapter is reserved to bring all of you fellow Maritime Law lovers an almost-complete list of the higher education institutions that provide a Maritime Law degree. This list consists of 34 schools across 4 continents that have impeccable nautical programs. Just turn to the next page to set sail to your future education!

NORTH AMERICA

Dalhousie Law School
    Location: Halifax, Nova Scotia
    Degree: LLM in Marine &
            Environmental Law
    Website:
www.dal.ca/faculty/law/melaw.html

Florida Coastal School of Law
    Location: Jacksonville, Florida
    Degree: LLM in Logistics &
            Transportation Law
    Website: www.llmcertification.com/llm-
logistics-and-transportation.html

St. Thomas University School of Law
    Location: Miami Gardens, Florida
    Degree: Maritime Law Society
    Website:
www.stu.edu/law/academics/student-
organizations/mls.html

EUROPE

Panthéon-Assas University
Location: Paris, France
Degree: LLM in International, Business
or Private Law with Marine
Law Courses
Website: www.sorbonne-assas-ils.org/

University of Nice Sophia Antipolis
Location: Nice, France
Degree: LLM in Marine and
Environmental Law
Website:
www.polytech.unice.fr/en/masters.html

University of Western Brittany in Brest
Location: Brest, Brittany, France
Degree: LLM in Marine Law
Website:
www.univ-
brest.fr/GB/menu/Research/Marine-
Science

International Maritime Law Institute
   Location: Tal-Qroqq, Msida, Malta
   Degree: LLM in International Maritime
      Law
   Website: www.imli.org/

Erasmus University Rotterdam
   Location: Rotterdam, Netherlands
   Degree: LLM in Business, Corporate,
      and Maritime Law, Master of
      Science in Maritime
      Economics and Logistics
   Website:
www.eur.nl/en/post-master/maritime-
economics-and-logistics

University of Oslo, Scandinavian Institute
of Maritime Law
   Location: Oslo, Norway
   Degree: LLM in Maritime Law
   Website:
www.uio.no/english/studies/programmes
/maritime-master/

University of Oslo
   Location: Oslo, Norway
   Degree: Master of Laws in Maritime
         Law
   Website:
www.uio.no/english/studies/programmes
/maritime-master/

Comillas Pontifical University, ICADE –
Spanish Maritime Institute
   Location: Madrid, Spain
   Degree: Master in Maritime Business
         and Maritime Law
   Website:
www.comillas.edu/en/postgrado-
propio/juridica/master-en-negocio-y-
derecho-maritimo-en

Bangor University
    Location: Bangor, Wales, UK
    Degree: LLM in Maritime Law, LLM in
        Law of the Sea
    Website:
www.bangor.ac.uk/courses/postgraduate/l
aw-of-the-sea-llm

Cardiff University
    Location: Cardiff, Wales, UK
    Degree: LLM in Shipping Law
    Website:
www.cardiff.ac.uk/study/postgraduate/tau
ght/courses/course/shipping-law-llm

City University London
    Location: London, England, UK
    Degree: LLM in Maritime Law
    Website:
www.city.ac.uk/courses/postgraduate/mar
itime-law

Liverpool John Moores University
    Location: Liverpool, England, UK
    Degree: BSc & MSc in Maritime,
        Transport & Logistics with
        embedded Maritime Law
        Elements
    Website:
www.ljmu.ac.uk/study/courses/postgradu
ates/maritime-operations

Queen Mary, University of London
    Location: London, England, UK
    Degree: LLM in International Shipping
        Law
    Website:
www.qmul.ac.uk/law/postgraduate/course
s/items/138030.html

Swansea University, Institute of
International Shipping and Trade Law
    Location: Swansea, Wales, UK
    Degree: LLM in International Maritime
        Law
    Website:
www.swansea.ac.uk/postgraduate/taught/l
aw/llmininternationalmaritimelaw/

CONTRIBUTORS!

This section is a HUGE 'Thank you!' to all of the
people on Twitter who believed in us:

@danguer21
@dangitshiep
@DylanTeeBH
@TheGrantDavis
@ComplexHormones
@ShirleySTANson
@sjwift1e
@annieclarkdt
@marimolina385
@angxlr
@YoJoeBow
@virginsupport69
@notcarsonhill
@nochillpatrick
@That1Girl_Kelsi
@juicyjuliak
@cuttothefeelin
@AndAwllThatJazz
@bellabilello
@FAGSafety
@sehunslittleslu
@hannesolo
@markstwotter
@glitchmood
@drewphilips_
@eriklulilian
@Taniaxlee
@PikaSchleh
@numbertrains
@EsmahSultan
@nico_giambanco
@pinkdyemonddd
@bomsmedication
@LeichtGreta
@inthenexttlife
@haydenremingto1
@EricDeLyrios
@Castiel203
@DaultonVenglar
@jboogie53175
@VeryHighandGay

@ashleeenic0le
@Mervin34073421
@ZacharyZahand
@APabloIsForever
@RoiPetite
@TempestKey
@iamasadmess
@EmojiRobinson
@Ed_Nunezz
@LEVYMENASSE
@pigeon_island
@edgardjceja
@smule77
@MyriamG999
@JustJoeyLopez
@connorcamper
@heavensclit
@finnriss
@johnmyhre
@the_ari_gato
@augusttmua
@yungbrujo
@saraislewd
@SilksAndSaddles
@CasMcFox
@LilBodyBigThoty
@woodydrawzz
@utahbj
@tpralex
@Give_Em_Bell
@Sameruu
@Demon_Dayz24
@half_orphan
@isabellathurk21
@DaveTorrex
@SchALovelyFace
@aliraza312
@MidnigthAnimal
@zipper_nation
@SplooginMelugin
@ech0brav0

@BhadFhattie
@shannpenn
@anthonyad8
@gaytorontocub
@nicksaladbar
@theuglymodel
@okzach_
@kc0872
@Simply_Named
@Davidioviga
@AmIAGirlDeluxe
@Pr_incorporated
@its_LeviOsa_
@lukehaller
@Jadacxnt
@killithme
@demisaysstuff
@AggieDave
@swedishfanboyy
@me1_Yee
@ja_caicai
@lunafxnction
@sobstori
@TheFirecestGay
@sheenkell
@LilSlurper
@gaycobs
@AlanSMartino
@eliotleeyt
@jessemorgunn
@kenetteray
@MatyKatz
@natalieolson27
@maddymrc
@20sumnvagaybond
@JorgeinOntario
@colder
@TammzBurruh
@helmitoimela
@gracenleann
@cholixbox1

@_kendryck
@JosephVasquezzz
@Judahaleyyy
@cruelcherries
@booranmiller
@just__amber1920
@AmwFreshprince
@6agonal
@historyboy71
@slutbot
@Tyrus__Goodrich
@KeannenMorgan
@adollopofdaisyy
@MWRIGHT286
@edgargierbolini
@aarndavd
@sassyjoshle
@hatchsarah15
@johnsongrass04
@gothliberace
@mnm_mia7
@bloomshaka
@sodafruit_
@BetterBullpen
@mulletorchestra
@ResVGA
@FargoJared
@AndieDeutschle
@maddieh8910
@ryan_orozco
@noXpiration
@ultraartdeco
@TIGERTAE
@blair80808
@hostileaf
@abbigansen
@margreatt
@dvd938
@_Alrexnader
@maxkile
@Rodriguez_5000
@pauli_xcx
@jriftedout
@jsguffey
@AnessaSparks
@PianySpots
@TwinSleepyGrins

@MariannaGibson
@prose0rose
@isaac_dailey
@RyHalvorsen
@MilkDermant
@MurseDad
@2lison
@pamoutsold
@dairyqueeef
@qwerty_magician
@KTognetti
@santiagorosal
@freebussy
@therealtedmarsh
@rbnelson77
@LipsJaden2018
@musgraves_stan
@colexcx1
@DylanDougal
@Gem_Girl_Gemma
@ice__cream__man
@mbrockjohnson
@BitnerLance
@akaryyy
@SandraBulcock
@Aly_Baske
@joshuavangogh
@NizarHadeli
@Laykin_xoxo
@bec_beckk
@NathanAllenHunt
@kululu45
@angelbbyray
@g_mamerica
@damn_it_damon
@danieldorable
@daringglenn
@sergioyaelnav
@De_done88
@alexiag20
@ladygodga
@sweetenerkev
@xofamemonster
@manilaluzbian
@ThanksGina
@_brianna_2_
@plantitasagrada

@doom__days
@HannahThird
@ChrisWeekly
@witchyboipop
@teemaction
@poppyschic
@Ewout1985
@keegancassin
@__sxif
@just_jake1994
@crdn9
@grace_balderas
@DarthXavier
@Jaloma_Pune
@lacroixboye
@heyitsmektj
@kcy_l
@gayandshook
@thatcarsonkid
@OmoAshley
@christine_tom2
@DietSkaw
@McSweez
@llots_e
@balmaincrocs
@YVANA___
@aphroditeswhore
@gargantuanrat
@tyler_b_123
@myregardslizzie
@bagelisfeeling
@Lone_Red_Rover
@Zeroroin
@KaeyaneMartinez
@XicoChicanx
@zvenya_
@ANGUSRAZE
@nuala_25
@tiersa_hawkes
@uploadanimalvid
@GrayFox814
@passionpitt
@JackShriver23
@ramirezalexa94
@trnsgrlfelicity
@NajkrajsiStromy
@quinn_mullany

@pecamp18
@gawky_angel
@g_davies24
@emilynm41
@adelyphant
@dorkoramadesign
@JRHensley12
@sfvis1
@gerardozunigat
@krysdelrey
@rhinoceruu
@VERSTINA
@DexterClift
@Maxine_Rhode
@sugarpinkmiss
@joeyfertig
@RussoKatie
@AlbertoSier
@rizzosardonicus
@SAINTEMRY
@AwesomeCarbajal
@candellewaxxx
@rheannasmith1
@lacabezadeluis
@LustForCola
@namgungcinema
@moi_boi7
@ConnerrM
@Aiurare
@fibsterss
@colinburnss
@nintendomad888
@smallshua
@chrisholmez
@joecandle
@DavidRyan091
@MatthewFussen
@KhaleesiKenna
@colechism
@Aristopoppy1
@robbxx2
@cgaertner_32
@_dylansaunders
@ItsJuhulian
@SmallGov4All
@_thetrashqueen
@GUNSWEEDLIBERTY

@j_cheta
@dannngerous
@Moonsault1814
@jordannskyee
@jenoutloud13
@lloraleii
@jacobiandersoni
@aileendiaries
@electrichapel
@Sui_Lovett
@___kati___
@m_stever
@offbrndlacroix
@leilamattie
@immmaterialboy
@twerk_uwu
@putawaythecrack
@ohheyitsalexi
@cdgrom
@ChiefJosheola
@haleyYAYgrr
@TylerJuh
@fabwboy
@AbbyAbby_JoyJoy
@FatimaGelani
@PlumFukt
@rodstevenglass
@AyeeRave
@ryleigh_eve
@QueenSatta
@zach618
@itsBRIAN_BTICH
@MorganRebecka
@SLEEPSmusic
@_caste_luis
@fundaydem
@yesimcaleb
@heyhaley98
@WanderlustGay
@Stvtistic
@thatsobrittney
@AkashSmarts
@stopxregina
@noahlynn
@tropicaldreamms
@urlmahone
@FancyBotwin

@JakeSteele46
@TheLeadSeener
@luanneplatter
@meceyyy
@lysticality
@kelvinclifton
@DarkVesperia
@londonbridge_ry
@Joeywendtwhere
@itsmargoat
@_scyne
@InnerDaddyIssue
@Emanuelvision
@kiwikinley
@christianfrey00
@ohhh_dannyboy
@Jakie46
@tinymilks
@gasstationsusie
@RaymieLayce
@carolinedippy
@fabwboy
@thecoastt
@cumdr0p
@joshb1224
@princessxace
@yikesitsheather
@horrorfess
@honeygrrl99
@RoberCharles95
@AsyRoughhh
@erickoctavius
@atlantian22
@tylerpmiranda
@Capafresco
@merbitches
@luzgoose_
@scarylcve
@MistyPurpleLake
@Nayyyuh
@kylemdub
@tinveniam
@____DAZE____
@ijustgobycam
@rbbbyy
@zachriaul
@jadelizabethhh

@roygaybiv
@SerenaSonoma
@F466OT
@oreofortune
@sadliluglyboy
@TheoTheThumb
@XenaZeitgeist
@harianakink
@pierre_wanga
@Powsean
@NotChrisWhited
@BBfanVoice2
@jjs999jjs
@finnalitas
@shabeasta
@sobiewankenobi
@pasteboi
@aaroncburstein
@Thoanos
@skinner28d
@kingkkade
@cseymour64
@sheeabriii
@unlockIt
@hrob508
@nameisjustice
@papakitty
@ZanDoyle
@duaoutsolddd
@mbretiagron
@camalexander4
@frigaythe13th
@abbywoww
@danksyrinna
@omannyte
@AOGCLOTHINGCO13
@j0sephharrison
@amadahasson
@AceOfTheWest
@tay_for_dayss
@zschutzy
@TeddyHoesevelt
@carbonfloppy
@stopthestatic
@_sammsanchez
@javredsox
@ohkayjayleen

@_malibu1992
@brnwld
@danjcotter
@badandbrookie
@Welpxx
@HEATHERREMO
@cutiebaek1
@billymelvin
@lukeuriah
@kevinbargerr
@sasha_ruby_
@loouaye
@Walunacy
@Myers_Mirabella
@bustedew
@TrashiGrande
@blameitonxcx
@dinnie_v
@j0hns0n_br0ck
@expelliariana
@Aerwiq
@LanaDelGaga123
@yambrobeyotch
@cahfee412
@BlueCocoNutz
@RichenTurner
@nicolenorth99
@chrixtineli
@henrykween
@GaspItsJess
@srslybrooklyne
@fricknfracksmom
@CuauhRL
@miaedn
@iJustinCross
@dezthoo
@OguzLuvsCookies
@Angelic39717031
@BurkeBobby
@ccakeblackwig
@ItsShawyane
@AustinPSmith96
@micksidol
@briecass
@bombshellfag
@kombuch_hoe
@Its_Kasey

@mbrandotommy
@nathanshinfeldt
@19dantheman81
@IsMiseAaron
@maxxioverdrive
@WVU_Katie
@kateybelle13
@mika_ljm
@byesexxual
@parton_tyler_
@merylwalker
@dav_ish
@frognerfrogner
@woodward_adam
@MyaaahCeee
@Jonnyboy_1
@__sacramental
@delicategaga
@MarsCottton
@bronaghcorona
@graciefromcali
@L0STMYPHONE
@sailorry
@kojibarnaby
@ImSoooHOLYfield
@taliadelrey
@gabba2018
@TeoMungaray
@cyber_metrix
@brittneylxnn
@claudiaelizaa54
@oduh_n
@meghan__orourke
@KimboJeremy
@guccigraceb
@vivamiley
@Sequins4Thought
@okniicole
@galacticskjes
@muleseackles
@BlondeBoyblloom
@teasoakedletter
@j_leunis
@ejski10
@artfulgold
@betz_trevor
@mylesbleu3

@G_U_M_D_R_O_P
@brunchbitchin
@SIDNEYNSFW
@dustinwaine
@DJHIMERA
@TYxHATT
@chalkycandy
@gaycowboyy
@JohnJoh88594467
@_andreuhhhh
@mhickstape
@gumixcx
@harsh_femme
@connordinary
@leeyuuhhhh
@kelleykingless
@ParissRain
@idiotnoises
@poppyismychurch
@heyolsport
@cpalomino13
@apollosdust
@cade_sierra
@swansonnn_
@noangelmp3
@justalilanal
@RyanDougandthom
@torrey_miller3
@MM_Cochran
@mr_rogers2013
@carlobyrd23
@abby_edra
@jayjkennedy
@Itshailshey
@LILLESSALONE
@s_richards28
@_samayab
@zeefizzy_
@iitsjustzac
@mhespinoza4
@izzy_turnerr
@gomez_ozy
@daryl_reed
@TarynAnnie
@xeepo
@daulton27
@Orruses

@HoKay_OhKay
@ClosetedFlop
@setheboi
@lovemac15
@NEEDS0MECRACK
@preciosa304
@sierraa_bennett
@warpfactorfunk
@homoawayfrmhome
@jesuscience
@VictoriaToffoli
@kenleemills
@kylie__wiley
@steviee_29
@doofuslucas
@kenmcguinnass
@maryjeanbud
@Rachleliz24
@MexicanNinjaaaa
@gen_joane
@YourFriendEmmy
@jeffmayy
@mariemng14
@DDonason
@ZackCochranTX
@lumiipon
@webzbaby
@iitsjustzac
@CaseyBunge
@Valatthedisco
@brooklynxbabe
@kinson_k
@BarkleyAdam
@abjectapathy
@mencomott
@immattjohnston
@off_twink
@NickGagama
@supergirlnusa
@sondrescactus
@AHSQuiznos
@johann_palo
@crybabyshark
@JamesCrabb
@the_miss_fitz
@Ajwest415
@tinydragonqueen

@fmnst_klljy
@SamiPliego
@FerneliusHunter
@DennisHou
@kimk4y1
@thatgirlj13
@johnsonvalerie9
@lillizzivert
@NickBelcher97
@aiyhonestly
@zzzzackary
@peppa_whore
@rnbwcloud
@peters629
@joyjoyjoyfuljoy
@caleb_walk
@sophitilla
@McMak__
@Adrian__Leos
@mlcary
@GannonNash
@katelabrujaja
@ocapolupo
@bbecccaaa
@tylerhahn21
@PriceBrittanie
@scarletstar
@brinleeboo
@uaenujsing
@GilroyBand
@titzer_layne
@Lesleygsmith3
@greatgabbsty
@carleekostowicz
@peachyounces
@ccaseylh
@Kaylee_DeMarchi
@JuanxUchis
@lilbodybigthoty
@dickridefoeva
@helautou
@apradical2
@Adam0_0l
@debbiedayglo
@hailey_tomko
@snglbuddy
@singularnewt

@yerawizerdlarry
@chipferrerer
@coolstorybita
@idleseon
@laikuho07
@MalloryMalvitz
@plxnted
@TravisJohnston2
@HiltonTrevor
@AmandaDamelio
@worktheclint
@alexanderhuafei
@awksosa
@raquelzuniga95
@meqansimm551
@julia_button
@sjscarbrough99
@DaryenGoesRawra
@Im_sarahbeth
@deekie
@jackuhlyneeyo
@egginramen
@jplusr10
@marqy018
@joaoemmelo
@SGUYBRAY
@poodlelashes98
@IamMike_L
@itsdalv
@nate_stev
@katiykat9
@fabb_ab
@chrisscottinman
@ohfuckimsorry
@tropithot
@LBENyandthejets
@eriq2500
@nguyennahg
@cringeytwink
@lolteag
@shayna_rose8
@justtimmy1
@kaemannnn
@sydseurer
@dalerkerr
@akakeyla
@spudski76

@RhanjellV
@PatrickRosemond
@jacobdoesmakeup
@rocka_Bri_lly
@hope_harlow
@anniekrenik
@lukeylux
@PhilipBrownJr
@beachfuneral_
@makenzipomaikai
@_lisigh
@allisonlynn_
@HectorNeustart
@JakeGThrasher
@bnxlvrd
@krisgraham99
@martinislip
@Levi_Sanders
@LincolnMondy
@AllPraiseB2Chad
@NEONEAL
@lina6005
@JRushR
@andys629
@witchassery
@c0dypendent
@myunapologeticd
@cashi17
@jocelyndavila97
@CodyElDreamer_
@_KatCo_
@creepain
@morcascr1s
@not_thisagainn
@jayjackson0516
@beccannelbert
@CaspianZee
@liambolz
@NoraBoraLora
@noboysx2remix
@badtakemachine
@gagaftflorence
@babyyykennn
@ilyood
@MaloneyHugh
@RJFl0yd
@feracobama12

@_alpphha
@dxvidcc
@monstersfollowu
@AnthGeek
@abxmo
@gabbanasss
@Smarmcharm
@sethpotter
@tavoferrer11
@evilfagg
@melricaaa_
@ChristianMGil
@__okkayla__
@awkwardabby1
@DCHomos
@holleywoodsigns
@Marceylina_M
@POP2stan
@LScudera
@p_nastay
@tswiftxcx
@sarahheathh
@JoeDubhGlas
@wowitswild
@katiy_helou
@PuppySinging
@emilyymichellen
@erynelb0n
@ParchedB
@j_il_l
@AJerund
@fggttingz
@LMAOOOOOOOOO
@Saundra_R
@Moooomlly
@MsNicoleCage
@kelsiebrownn
@jen_naparker
@jenn_m_meyer
@sarcastita
@ashrebecky
@marstheart
@SelfAbstract
@angelato__
@goingistough
@hombrepdx
@corinnebowerss

@abbydoug_
@ProfChestnut
@aperiodjperiodb
@BPtheGasStation
@camilogotbandz
@kennapott
@masqurade95
@mvo_marilyn
@henryschwartzz
@LoneKokiri
@deadboydanny
@becca_laser
@123letsgoobitch
@berumenelena
@DeadnGay
@it_me_G
@Emiasly
@AmyMarie2713
@TayVanDev
@kristen_disbrow
@gdgbkdds
@98HOODLUM
@zryan721
@vapourboy
@SethET96
@dar_squared
@joannesbitch
@TCVass
@eriinmariie23
@Bi_Laws
@LyssaDope
@HumanGrackle
@LuisFZulu
@dvnots
@Daftzak
@hxneymxxninn
@jasonwendtwhere
@charisisforlove
@thursdaypilots
@jacefaceluxe
@dustinduong
@DJMALSONIDO
@jvanboxtel13
@amayogoody1
@gabegnz
@fancy_fag
@cigabear93

@GigiActress
@seafoxxart
@pettyethiopian
@unsweetbish
@Mocking17
@pr3ssr3wind3
@Leshawna13
@campodonicoo_
@lilres
@Dear_Jonny
@megan_walker_14
@ejcthe2nd
@_PatriciaLemon
@LalalaVieEnSolo
@CloudAtlas0222
@rmando11_
@fatchedda___
@acballerina15
@theabstinence
@Tylorda
@SonofMunin
@JogaDrunk
@rightmovement
@lysergicdelight
@jensen_goldfine
@lily_bbeatrice
@xohiills
@thefuckingbicth
@theatersivan
@lovelythebands
@Pugs_of_Clari
@brandon_oneal_
@whatbritta
@patdaddy33
@JakeBurkhalter4
@averayray
@jibihimo
@JonathanWittman
@Josh2762
@ConnorCorbin2
@MyaHorak
@lxasta
@crookedvanessa
@karynnedenise
@urvipatella
@holdthameyo
@barker_grace

@SubtleAlcoholic
@OmfgSheFknDed
@itsaliamm
@AshleeBrianne97
@ohhibrandon
@chekhovzgun
@Savannah_McP
@PaulFitz1983
@QueerMystic7
@RMellinger69
@broke_wizard_
@mattlovesrays
@badrobot68
@the_ryanoserous
@helloitsmeJenna
@GiovanniALC
@klingj72
@brbehh
@camspoe
@mediocraly
@murraywow
@raphaelvezga
@_notmariah
@number1coochie
@tims_ferguson
@JonathanYoungxo
@dmeredith2
@HollandAlaina
@ItWasntLove
@Lauren99611165
@Brandon_Lay
@belbyshincoe
@sj0b3rg
@Momma_Mallory
@Saaac7
@pocaro_
@maddiecruc
@stevenikolakis
@dianaasilla
@ruffboiz
@sparkupbuzzcut
@elijah_lee_king
@01_Boxer
@ProfProvolone
@dderbb
@cwizzle97
@christiankosman

@emmashores16

@kat_fraz2

@JOkoorian

@meredankmemes

@proud_mama_hoe

@sarahlynncole

@lexyryg

@jstroud97

@tyjahansteele

@melysantos2

@mascbaby

@FENTYSAMUEL

@Taylor__Oneal

@izzygazette

@chaneln0fag

@selenasdong

@JovannaGerardo

@indielead

@osborne_aj

@kephlexy

@sigh_curious

@eattheflan

@oli_wolfe

@itsroloo

@kaychalla

@claremlachnik

@hostilespice

@thegeissberger

@katieelbert_

@RealJorgeAro

@BlueGreenBooks1

ABOUT THE AUTHORS

Author Connor Gleim conducting Maritime Law research

Connor Gleim received his Doctor of Philosophy Degree from the World Admiralty University in Malmö, Sweden. While completing his degree, Gleim worked with the United Nations to establish a more concrete Maritime Law structure in Scandinavia. His research and presentation on the United Nations Convention on the Law of the Ocean is set to release in 2020. In the meantime, he will be sailing the sea with his wife – Deb – also a graduate of WAU. They reside in Flekke, Norway.

Author Austin Robinson conducting Maritime Law research

Austin Robinson received his Master of Law Degree from Dollhouse University in Halifax, Nova Scotia, where he worked as a Nautical Care Partner for Flying Fish Law Firm concurrently. He has numerous legal accomplishments fighting justice in the Private Ocean Disputes Court. His favorite activities include educating children at elementary schools about the ocean, doing pro bono work for poor seamen, and – of course – fishing on the shores of Halifax!

Author Patrick Golden in front of a Blockbuster

Patrick Golden received his Geriatric Nurse Practitioner certification after serving 20 years in the United States Navy. While stationed on the seaside of many impoverished countries, Golden discovered his love of geriatric nursing when he started treating the native elders for sea-related sicknesses. Upon leaving the Navy, Golden attended Warden University for his GNP certification. He currently travels with Geriatric Nurses Without Borders across North Africa, the Arabian Peninsula, and the islands surrounding Southeast Asia. He has cured thousands of elders with sea sickness!

Made in the USA
Middletown, DE
11 August 2023